Melania: A Critical Review of Melania Trump Book—
Enigma, Icon, or Political Bystander.

By Callum Ellis

Dedication Page

To the curious minds seeking to understand the people shaping our world.

Acknowledgment Page

Writing this review was a journey shaped by countless discussions, insights, and observations. I extend my gratitude to the readers, friends, and thought leaders who continue to inspire me to explore literature critically. Special thanks to the author of *MELANIA* for providing a thought-provoking work worthy of review and reflection.

Table of Contents

Introduction: A Glimpse into a Private Life

Melania Trump's memoir, *Melania*, offers readers an intimate look into her life, from her early years in Slovenia to her tenure as First Lady of the United States. The book delves into her personal experiences, beliefs, and the challenges she faced under the public's scrutiny.

Themes

1. **Identity and Self-Representation**: Throughout the memoir, Melania seeks to define herself beyond the public's perception. She addresses misconceptions about her marriage and personal beliefs, aiming to present a more nuanced image of herself.

2. **Public Perception and Media Scrutiny**: The book highlights the intense media attention she received, particularly during her husband's presidency. She discusses how public scrutiny affected her and her family, offering insights into the challenges of maintaining privacy in the public eye.

3. **Intersection of Politics and Personal Life**: Melania reflects on the blending of her personal life with her role as First Lady. She shares her experiences navigating political events, public appearances, and the expectations placed upon her, providing a candid look at the complexities of her position.

4. **Impact of Media Representation**: The memoir addresses how the media portrayed her, often focusing on her silence and demeanor. She offers

her perspective on these portrayals, discussing the impact they had on her and her family's lives.

Writing Style

Melania's writing is straightforward and reflective, with a tone that balances personal anecdotes with broader reflections. The narrative is structured chronologically, allowing readers to follow her journey from childhood to her time in the White House. While the prose is accessible, some critics have noted that the memoir lacks depth in certain areas, particularly concerning her marriage and political views.

Author's Intentions

Melania appears intent on reshaping her public image and providing a personal account of her life. By addressing rumors and misconceptions, she aims to offer a more accurate portrayal of her experiences and beliefs. The memoir serves as a platform for her to express her views on various topics, including her stance on abortion rights and her reaction to the FBI raid on their Mar-a-Lago estate.

Sociopolitical Context

Published in October 2024, the memoir arrives at a time when Melania's husband, Donald Trump, has been re-elected as President. This context is significant, as it provides a backdrop for her reflections on their time in the White House and the political climate of the era. The book also touches on contemporary issues such as media representation, public scrutiny, and the role of women in politics, offering insights into the challenges faced by public figures in the modern age.

Impact on Public Perception

Melania has sparked discussions about the former First Lady's role and influence. While some readers appreciate her candidness and the personal insights she provides, others feel the memoir does not delve deeply enough into certain aspects of her life and marriage. Nonetheless, the book contributes to the broader conversation about the expectations and realities of public figures, particularly women in politics.

Significance in Contemporary Literature

As a political memoir, *Melania* offers a unique perspective from a First Lady who maintained a relatively low public profile during her husband's presidency. It adds to the genre by providing personal anecdotes and reflections that humanize a figure often seen through a political lens. The memoir's candid approach to sensitive topics, such as her son's health and her personal beliefs, adds depth to the discourse on the intersection of personal and public life.

Strengths

- **Personal Insights**: The memoir offers a rare glimpse into Melania Trump's personal life, providing readers with a deeper understanding of her experiences and challenges.

- **Candid Reflections**: She addresses various rumors and misconceptions, offering her perspective on events and decisions that shaped her public image.

Weaknesses

- **Limited Political Analysis**: Some critics note that the memoir lacks in-depth analysis of her political views and the complexities of her marriage, leaving certain areas unexplored.

- **Surface-Level Exploration**: While the memoir touches on significant events, it sometimes offers only a surface-level exploration, leaving readers wanting more detailed accounts.

In conclusion, *Melania* provides a personal account of a woman who navigated the complexities of public life with grace and determination. While it offers valuable insights into her experiences and beliefs, it also leaves certain areas unexplored, prompting readers to seek a more comprehensive understanding of her life and role in contemporary society.

politics, offering insights into the challenges faced by public figures in the modern age.

Impact on Public Perception

Melania has sparked discussions about the former First Lady's role and influence. While some readers appreciate her candidness and the personal insights she provides, others feel the memoir does not delve deeply enough into certain aspects of her life and marriage. Nonetheless, the book contributes to the broader conversation about the expectations and realities of public figures, particularly women in politics.

Significance in Contemporary Literature

As a political memoir, *Melania* offers a unique perspective from a First Lady who maintained a relatively low public profile during her husband's presidency. It adds to the genre by providing personal anecdotes and reflections that humanize a figure often seen through a political lens. The memoir's candid approach to sensitive topics, such as her son's health and her personal beliefs, adds depth to the discourse on the intersection of personal and public life.

Strengths

- **Personal Insights**: The memoir offers a rare glimpse into Melania Trump's personal life, providing readers with a deeper understanding of her experiences and challenges.

- **Candid Reflections**: She addresses various rumors and misconceptions, offering her perspective on events and decisions that shaped her public image.

Weaknesses

- **Limited Political Analysis**: Some critics note that the memoir lacks in-depth analysis of her political views and the complexities of her marriage, leaving certain areas unexplored.

- **Surface-Level Exploration**: While the memoir touches on significant events, it sometimes offers only a surface-level exploration, leaving readers wanting more detailed accounts.

In conclusion, *Melania* provides a personal account of a woman who navigated the complexities of public life with grace and determination. While it offers valuable insights into her experiences and beliefs, it also leaves certain areas unexplored, prompting readers to seek a more comprehensive understanding of her life and role in contemporary society.

Chapter 1 – Roots in Slovenia from *Melania* by Melania Trump

In Chapter 1 of *Melania*, titled "Roots in Slovenia," the narrative embarks on a reflective exploration of the author's early years in a modest, Communist-era Slovenia. Melania Trump, born Melania Knavs, paints a picture of her upbringing in Sevnica, a small town surrounded by the picturesque Sava River. From the outset, this chapter provides a foundational understanding of the forces that shaped her character—her family, her environment, and the political landscape.

Themes: Identity and Early Resilience

The most prominent theme in this chapter is the shaping of Melania's identity through the lens of her Slovenian roots. Raised in a working-class family with a car dealer father and a textile factory worker mother, Melania offers a glimpse into her humble beginnings. The Communist regime that governed her early years added a layer of complexity to her experiences. The tension between this political environment and Melania's drive for a more glamorous, international life is a key dynamic that runs throughout her early years.

Melania's reflection on her early life touches on the resilience that was instilled in her from a young age. The chapter highlights how her modest background did not limit her aspirations. It suggests that Melania's ability to navigate her way from Slovenia to international fame is deeply rooted in the values of independence and ambition cultivated during her formative years.

Writing Style: Introspective yet Detached

Melania's writing style in this chapter is a mixture of introspection and detached observation. While she provides personal insights into her family life and upbringing, there is a sense of distance between her younger self and the present-day author. This detachment can be interpreted as a deliberate choice to maintain a certain level of privacy and control over the narrative. The writing feels more like a retrospective analysis, where the author reflects on her past from a place of experience, rather than actively engaging with the raw emotions of the time.

This choice may appeal to readers who are seeking a more polished, controlled portrayal of Melania's journey. However, it also risks alienating those looking for a more visceral or emotional connection with the subject matter. The writing, while precise and measured, lacks the immediacy or vividness that could have made the portrayal of her early life more compelling.

Author's Intentions: Framing a Foundation for Future Ambitions

In terms of authorial intent, Chapter 1 functions as a blueprint for understanding how Melania's upbringing influenced her later achievements. By emphasizing her humble beginnings and the circumstances under which she grew up, Melania presents herself as someone who overcame adversity. The rural backdrop of Slovenia, coupled with her modest family life, underscores her evolution into an ambitious and internationally recognized figure.

The chapter sets the stage for Melania's journey into the world of modeling, which serves as a metaphor for breaking free from her provincial roots. The author seems keen to establish a narrative that highlights her autonomy and self-determination, offering readers an early understanding of how her background shaped her future decisions.

Sociopolitical Context: A Reflection of Yugoslav and Post-Communist Influence

From a sociopolitical perspective, Chapter 1 provides valuable context for understanding the Yugoslav backdrop in which Melania's early years were shaped. The Communist regime in Slovenia at the time played a significant role in limiting personal freedom and shaping the economic landscape. In this environment, Melania's ambition and eventual move to the West could be seen as symbolic of a desire for autonomy and escape from a constrained system.

At the same time, the chapter subtly hints at the broader shifts happening in Eastern Europe during the 1980s and 1990s, with the fall of Communism and the opening of new political and economic doors for those like Melania seeking opportunities beyond their borders. The personal narrative, thus, functions as a microcosm of the larger sociopolitical upheavals happening in Europe at the time.

Impact on Public Perception and Contemporary Literature

In terms of public perception, this chapter of *Melania* serves as a carefully curated introduction to the author's life. By focusing on her early years and framing them within the context of modesty and resilience, Melania seeks to establish an image of self-made success. For those unfamiliar with her background, the chapter provides a humanizing glimpse into the beginnings of a figure who would later become a global sensation.

However, it's worth noting that some readers may find the lack of emotional depth in this chapter to be a limiting factor. While Melania succeeds in providing factual details and constructing a coherent narrative, the absence of a deeper emotional connection with the audience may diminish the chapter's potential impact. Critics of the book might argue that this lack of vulnerability prevents readers from fully engaging with the author on a personal level, making it more difficult to relate to her story.

Strengths and Weaknesses

The strengths of Chapter 1 lie in its ability to establish the foundations of Melania's character and aspirations. Her background, particularly her upbringing in Slovenia, is presented as a pivotal influence on her later success. The precision of the writing allows for a clear and concise account of her early years, while the focus on her resilience and independence provides a strong basis for understanding her later decisions.

However, the weaknesses of the chapter include the aforementioned emotional distance and lack of vivid narrative detail. While the chapter is informative, it lacks the kind of emotional immediacy that could have made Melania's story more engaging and compelling. For a reader unfamiliar with her background, the chapter may feel more like a factual recounting than a deeply personal narrative.

Conclusion

In conclusion, Chapter 1 of *Melania* provides a solid foundation for understanding the author's early life in Slovenia. Through the lens of her modest upbringing, Melania introduces key themes of resilience, ambition, and the drive to break free from her provincial roots. While the writing style may not resonate with all readers due to its detached nature, the chapter serves its purpose in framing Melania's identity and setting the stage for the rest of the memoir. The sociopolitical context of Communist-era Slovenia adds an important layer to the narrative, positioning Melania's journey within a broader historical framework that informs her eventual rise to fame and prominence.

Chapter 2: The Journey to America

In Chapter 2 of *Melania*, titled "The Journey to America," the narrative takes a significant turn as it chronicles Melania Trump's ambitious move from Slovenia to the United States, marking a pivotal point in her life story. Building on the foundation established in Chapter 1, where her modest beginnings and early aspirations are detailed, this chapter focuses on the bold decision to pursue a career in modeling beyond the boundaries of her hometown.

Themes: Ambition and Reinvention

The central theme in this chapter is Melania's ambition to reinvent herself on a global stage. Her decision to leave Slovenia at the age of 26 was not just a career move, but a defining moment in her life—a moment that reflects her desire to escape the constraints of a provincial life and pursue something larger. While Slovenia offered her a safe, structured environment, the lure of international fame in Milan, Paris, and eventually New York proved irresistible.

This chapter emphasizes the theme of reinvention, as Melania is no longer just a girl from Sevnica but an ambitious young woman ready to carve out her future in the competitive world of fashion modeling. The move to America symbolizes her leap from a small European town to one of the most fast-paced, high-stakes cities in the world.

Writing Style: Aspirational and Reflective

The writing style in Chapter 2 is aspirational and reflective, with Melania using her narrative to convey the emotional complexity of such a monumental decision. The tone is measured and controlled, as she recounts her fears, hopes, and the challenges she faced when deciding to leave everything behind. Her reflections show a balance between excitement and trepidation, offering insight into the emotional conflict of stepping into the unknown.

The author also reflects on the cultural shock she experienced when she first arrived in Milan and later in Paris. These moments are recounted with a mixture of awe and determination, showing her resilience in adapting to a new lifestyle and language.

Author's Intentions: Framing Her Transformation

Through this chapter, Melania is not only recounting her personal journey but also framing it as a transformation—a reinvention that will take her from being a small-town girl in Communist-era Slovenia to a high-profile international model. The author's intentions are clear: to showcase her transformation into a self-made woman who sought opportunities beyond her origins. This chapter serves to set the stage for her eventual rise to fame and her introduction into the upper echelons of society.

By focusing on the early part of her career, the chapter aims to establish Melania as someone who, despite the odds, was determined to succeed and prove her worth in an industry that was often unforgiving. In doing so, she introduces herself as a figure driven by ambition, which later became a core part of her public persona.

Sociopolitical Context: The End of Communist Yugoslavia

From a sociopolitical standpoint, Chapter 2 also touches upon the historical context in which Melania's journey unfolded. Slovenia, during the time of her departure in the early 1990s, was still under the influence of the Yugoslav Federation. The region was undergoing significant political upheaval as it moved toward independence, which also meant economic and social uncertainty.

The decision to leave was, in part, a response to the shifting political climate. With the rise of nationalism and the breakup of Yugoslavia, Melania's choice to move to the West represents a desire for new opportunities—both personally and professionally. Her narrative is embedded within a broader historical moment that saw many individuals from former Eastern Bloc countries seeking better prospects in the West.

Impact on Public Perception and Contemporary Literature

Chapter 2 of *Melania* significantly impacts the way the public perceives Melania Trump. By highlighting her ambition and desire for reinvention, the chapter begins to build her image as a self-sufficient individual who took bold steps to shape her future. This sets her apart from other political figures and public personalities, giving her a sense of autonomy that many of her critics may overlook.

In terms of contemporary literature, the chapter serves as an example of how personal memoirs can provide insight into the motivations of public figures, particularly in the context of their career choices. It blends personal history with larger sociopolitical themes, providing both a portrait of an individual and a glimpse into the broader political shifts that shaped her life.

Strengths and Weaknesses

One of the strengths of Chapter 2 is its focus on the universal theme of ambition, which resonates with a wide range of readers. Melania's story of leaving behind everything she knew for the pursuit of a dream is relatable to anyone who has ever taken a leap of faith. The chapter succeeds in capturing the emotional complexity of such a decision, giving it depth and substance.

However, a potential weakness in the chapter lies in its limited exploration of the specific challenges Melania faced upon arriving in the West. While the narrative mentions her move to Milan and Paris, it lacks the raw details that could make her struggle more palpable. The challenges of being an immigrant in a foreign country, learning a new language, and navigating the often-difficult world of fashion could have been explored in more detail to deepen the reader's connection to her journey.

Chapter 3: Meeting Donald Trump

In Chapter 3 of *Melania*, titled "Meeting Donald Trump," the narrative delves into the serendipitous encounter between Melania Knauss and Donald Trump, a pivotal moment that would profoundly influence her personal and professional trajectory.

Themes: Serendipity and Personal Agency

This chapter underscores the themes of serendipity and personal agency. The chance meeting at a New York Fashion Week party in 1998, where Donald Trump, accompanied by another woman, approached Melania, highlights the unpredictable nature of life. Melania's decision to provide her phone number, rather than accepting his, exemplifies her assertiveness and control over her personal interactions. This act of agency set the stage for a relationship that would intertwine their lives in significant ways.

Writing Style: Anecdotal and Reflective

The writing style in this chapter is anecdotal and reflective, offering readers an intimate glimpse into the early stages of their relationship. Melania recounts the encounter with a blend of nostalgia and introspection, providing insights into her initial impressions of Donald Trump and the dynamics of their early interactions. The narrative is engaging, drawing readers into the unfolding story of their connection.

Author's Intentions: Humanizing a Public Figure

Through this chapter, the author aims to humanize Melania Trump by focusing on a personal and relatable experience—the beginning of a significant relationship. By sharing this intimate moment, the memoir seeks to present Melania not just as a public figure but as an individual with personal experiences and emotions. This approach allows readers to connect with her on a more personal level, beyond her roles in the public eye.

Sociopolitical Context: The Glamour of the 1990s Fashion Scene

The encounter took place during the vibrant and competitive fashion scene of the 1990s, a period marked by the prominence of supermodels and the burgeoning influence of media in shaping public perceptions. This context is significant, as it highlights the intersection of fashion, celebrity culture, and the personal lives of those involved. The fashion industry of that era was a microcosm of broader societal trends, including the commodification of personal relationships and the blending of personal and professional spheres.

Impact on Public Perception and Contemporary Literature

This chapter contributes to the public's understanding of Melania Trump by providing a personal narrative that contrasts with her more public persona. It offers a glimpse into her life before her marriage to Donald Trump, portraying her as a successful model navigating the complexities of relationships and career. In contemporary literature, such personal anecdotes are valuable for offering nuanced perspectives on public figures, moving beyond media portrayals to reveal the human experiences behind the headlines.

Strengths and Weaknesses

A strength of this chapter is its ability to convey the excitement and uncertainty of new relationships, making Melania's experience relatable to a wide audience. The detailed recounting of the initial meeting adds depth to her character, allowing readers to see her as more than a public figure. However, a potential weakness is the limited exploration of the challenges and complexities that may have arisen from their relationship, particularly given the public scrutiny they would later face. A more in-depth analysis of these aspects could provide a fuller understanding of their dynamic.

Chapter 4: Life in the Public Eye

In Chapter 4 of *Melania*, titled "Lights, Camera, Model," the narrative delves into Melania Trump's evolution from a young girl with a passion for fashion to an internationally recognized model. This chapter offers a comprehensive look at her modeling career, highlighting the challenges and triumphs that defined her journey in the public eye.

Themes: Ambition and Self-Discovery

The central themes of this chapter are ambition and self-discovery. Melania's early fascination with fashion, sparked at the age of six when she modeled her mother's designs, laid the groundwork for her future career. Her decision to pursue modeling professionally, despite the industry's competitive nature, underscores her determination and self-confidence. This chapter illustrates her relentless pursuit of success and personal growth, emphasizing her ability to navigate and thrive in the demanding world of fashion.

Writing Style: Reflective and Inspirational

The writing style in this chapter is reflective and inspirational. Melania recounts her experiences with a sense of gratitude and introspection, acknowledging the lessons learned and the personal growth achieved. The narrative is both engaging and motivational, offering readers insight into the mindset of a woman who overcame obstacles to achieve her dreams. Her reflections on the importance of hard work, resilience, and self-belief serve as a source of inspiration for those aspiring to succeed in their own endeavors.

Author's Intentions: Showcasing Personal Growth and Professionalism

Through this chapter, the author aims to showcase Melania Trump's personal growth and professionalism. By detailing her progression from local fashion shows in Slovenia to international runways, the memoir highlights her adaptability and commitment to excellence. The chapter serves to illustrate her evolution not only as a model but also as an individual who embraced new cultures and opportunities, reflecting her broader journey of self-discovery and empowerment.

Sociopolitical Context: The Global Fashion Industry

The sociopolitical context of the global fashion industry during the 1990s is significant in this chapter. The era was characterized by the dominance of supermodels and the increasing influence of media in shaping public perceptions. Melania's entry into this competitive field required navigating complex dynamics, including cultural differences, language barriers, and the pressures of maintaining a public image. Her success in this environment reflects her resilience and ability to adapt to the evolving demands of the fashion industry.

Impact on Public Perception and Contemporary Literature

This chapter contributes to the public's understanding of Melania Trump by providing a detailed account of her professional achievements and the dedication required to attain them. It humanizes her, portraying her as a hardworking and ambitious individual who pursued her dreams with determination. In contemporary literature, such personal narratives offer valuable insights into the lives of public figures, moving beyond media portrayals to reveal the complexities of their experiences and the factors that shaped their identities.

Strengths and Weaknesses

A strength of this chapter is its candid portrayal of the modeling industry, including the challenges faced and the resilience required to succeed. Melania's openness about her experiences provides readers with a nuanced understanding of the fashion world and her role within it. However, a potential weakness is the limited exploration of the personal sacrifices and ethical dilemmas encountered in the industry. A more in-depth analysis of these aspects could offer a fuller picture of the complexities involved in her career.

Chapter 5: The Role of First Lady

In Chapter 5 of *Melania*, titled "The Role of First Lady," Melania Trump offers an intimate portrayal of her tenure in the White House, providing readers with a nuanced understanding of her experiences and initiatives during this period.

Themes: Advocacy and Personal Reflection

The central themes of this chapter are advocacy and personal reflection. Melania discusses her commitment to various causes, notably the "Be Best" initiative, which focuses on combating cyberbullying, promoting children's health, and addressing the opioid crisis. She reflects on the challenges and rewards of championing these issues, highlighting her dedication to making a positive impact. Additionally, the chapter delves into her personal experiences and growth, offering insights into her role beyond the public eye.

Writing Style: Candid and Insightful

The writing style in this chapter is candid and insightful. Melania provides a transparent account of her experiences, sharing both the triumphs and difficulties she encountered. Her narrative is engaging, offering readers a window into the complexities of her role as First Lady. The chapter balances personal anecdotes with professional insights, creating a comprehensive portrayal of her time in the White House.

Author's Intentions: Humanizing the First Lady

Through this chapter, the author aims to humanize the role of First Lady, presenting Melania as a dedicated individual navigating the complexities of public service. By sharing her personal reflections and challenges, the memoir seeks to provide a deeper understanding of the responsibilities and experiences associated with this position. The chapter serves to highlight her commitment to her initiatives and her personal growth during her tenure.

Sociopolitical Context: The First Lady's Influence

The sociopolitical context of the First Lady's role is significant in this chapter. Traditionally, the First Lady serves as a figurehead for various social causes, often influencing public opinion and policy. Melania's initiatives, particularly "Be Best," reflect her approach to leveraging her position to address pressing societal issues. The chapter explores the dynamics of this role, including the public's expectations and the personal fulfillment derived from advocacy.

Impact on Public Perception and Contemporary Literature

This chapter contributes to the public's understanding of Melania Trump by providing a personal account of her time in the White House. It offers insights into her motivations and the challenges she faced, contributing to a more nuanced perception of her tenure. In contemporary literature, such personal narratives are valuable for offering perspectives on public figures, moving beyond media portrayals to reveal the complexities of their experiences.

Strengths and Weaknesses

A strength of this chapter is its openness in discussing the challenges and rewards of the First Lady role. Melania's candidness provides readers with a realistic portrayal of her experiences. However, a potential weakness is the limited exploration of the political and social controversies that occurred during her husband's presidency. A more in-depth analysis of these aspects could offer a fuller understanding of her role and the complexities involved.

Chapter 6: Personal Beliefs and Public Perception

In Chapter 6 of *Melania*, titled "Personal Beliefs and Public Perception," Melania Trump delves into her personal convictions and the challenges of maintaining her privacy amidst public scrutiny. This chapter offers readers a deeper understanding of her values and the complexities of her public image.

Themes: Privacy, Autonomy, and Advocacy

The central themes of this chapter are privacy, autonomy, and advocacy. Melania emphasizes the importance of personal privacy, particularly concerning her son, Barron, and her own beliefs. She discusses her commitment to protecting her family's privacy and the difficulties of balancing personal convictions with public expectations. Additionally, the chapter highlights her advocacy for women's rights, notably her support for reproductive rights, underscoring her belief in women's autonomy over their bodies and decisions.

Writing Style: Reflective and Assertive

The writing style in this chapter is reflective and assertive. Melania articulates her beliefs with clarity and conviction, providing readers with insight into her personal values and the challenges she faced in upholding them. The narrative is both introspective and forthright, offering a candid look at her experiences and the complexities of navigating public life while staying true to her principles.

Author's Intentions: Clarifying Personal Stances

Through this chapter, the author aims to clarify her personal stances on various issues, particularly women's rights and privacy. By openly discussing her beliefs and the challenges of maintaining privacy, Melania seeks to provide a more nuanced understanding of her character and motivations. The chapter serves to humanize her, portraying her as an individual with strong convictions navigating the complexities of public life.

Sociopolitical Context: Women's Rights and Public Scrutiny

The sociopolitical context of women's rights and public scrutiny is significant in this chapter. Melania's support for reproductive rights and her emphasis on women's autonomy reflect broader societal debates on these issues. Her experiences highlight the challenges public figures face in balancing personal beliefs with public expectations, especially when their views may not align with prevailing political narratives.

Impact on Public Perception and Contemporary Literature

This chapter contributes to the public's understanding of Melania Trump by providing a candid account of her personal beliefs and the challenges of maintaining privacy. It offers insights into her motivations and the complexities of her public image, contributing to a more nuanced perception of her character. In contemporary literature, such personal narratives are valuable for offering perspectives on public figures, moving beyond media portrayals to reveal the complexities of their experiences.

Strengths and Weaknesses

A strength of this chapter is its openness in discussing personal beliefs and the challenges of maintaining privacy. Melania's candidness provides readers with a realistic portrayal of her experiences and convictions. However, a potential weakness is the limited exploration of the broader political implications of her beliefs. A more in-depth analysis of how her personal convictions intersected with her husband's policies could offer a fuller understanding of her role and the complexities involved.

Chapter 7: Family Matters

In Chapter 7 of *Melania*, titled "Family Matters," Melania Trump offers an intimate look into her family life, emphasizing the importance of her roles as a wife and mother amidst the public scrutiny that accompanies her position.

Themes: Family, Privacy, and Resilience

This chapter delves into themes of family, privacy, and resilience. Melania discusses her dedication to providing a stable and nurturing environment for her son, Barron, and the challenges of safeguarding her family's privacy in the face of intense media attention. She reflects on the strength and unity within her family, highlighting the support they provide each other during times of public and personal challenges.

Writing Style: Personal and Reflective

The writing style in this chapter is personal and reflective. Melania shares anecdotes that reveal her deep commitment to her family's well-being and her efforts to maintain normalcy despite their public roles. Her narrative provides readers with a glimpse into the private moments that define her family life, offering a contrast to the often sensationalized portrayals in the media.

Author's Intentions: Humanizing the Public Persona

Through this chapter, Melania aims to humanize her public persona by showcasing her devotion to her family. By sharing personal stories and insights, she seeks to present herself not just as a former First Lady, but as a mother and wife who values her family's privacy and well-being above all else.

Sociopolitical Context: Navigating Public Life

The sociopolitical context of this chapter centers on the challenges of raising a family within the political spotlight. Melania addresses the difficulties of protecting her son from media scrutiny and the measures she takes to ensure his upbringing remains as unaffected as possible by their public status. She also touches upon the support system within her family that helps them navigate the pressures of public life.

Impact on Public Perception and Contemporary Literature

This chapter contributes to a more nuanced public perception of Melania Trump by highlighting her role as a dedicated mother and wife. In contemporary literature, such personal narratives offer valuable insights into the private lives of public figures, allowing readers to see beyond the public facade and understand the personal values and commitments that guide them.

Strengths and Weaknesses

A strength of this chapter is its candidness in discussing the challenges of maintaining family privacy amidst public scrutiny. Melania's reflections provide a relatable perspective on the universal desire to protect one's family. However, a potential weakness is the limited discussion on how her public role may have influenced her family's dynamics and the specific strategies employed to balance public duties with private life.

Chapter 8: Navigating Controversies

In Chapter 8 of *Melania*, titled "Navigating Controversies," Melania Trump addresses the various public controversies that arose during her tenure as First Lady, providing her perspective on these events and the challenges they presented.

Themes: Public Scrutiny, Misinterpretation, and Resilience

This chapter delves into themes of public scrutiny, misinterpretation, and resilience. Melania reflects on how her actions and statements were often subject to intense media attention and misinterpretation. She discusses the personal and public challenges of being in the spotlight and the resilience required to maintain her composure and focus amidst criticism.

Writing Style: Candid and Reflective

The writing style in this chapter is candid and reflective. Melania openly discusses her feelings and reactions to the controversies, providing readers with an intimate look at her personal experiences. Her narrative is introspective, offering insights into her thought processes and the lessons she learned from these challenges.

Author's Intentions: Clarifying Intentions and Addressing Misconceptions

Through this chapter, Melania aims to clarify her intentions behind certain actions and address common misconceptions. By providing her perspective, she seeks to offer a more nuanced understanding of the events that garnered public attention and to correct any misunderstandings about her motives and beliefs.

Sociopolitical Context: The Role of the First Lady and Media Dynamics

The sociopolitical context of this chapter centers on the role of the First Lady and the dynamics between public figures and the media. Melania's experiences highlight the challenges inherent in navigating public expectations and media scrutiny, particularly for individuals in prominent political positions. Her reflections offer insights into the pressures and responsibilities associated with the role of the First Lady.

Impact on Public Perception and Contemporary Literature

This chapter contributes to a more nuanced public perception of Melania Trump by providing her personal account of the controversies she faced. In contemporary literature, such narratives are valuable for offering insights into the personal experiences of public figures, allowing readers to understand the complexities of their roles and the challenges they encounter.

Strengths and Weaknesses

A strength of this chapter is its openness and honesty, as Melania does not shy away from discussing difficult topics and her personal reactions to them. However, a potential weakness is that some readers may find her explanations insufficient or may desire more detailed accounts of certain events. Additionally, while she addresses various controversies, the chapter may not fully explore the broader implications of these events on public discourse and political culture.

Chapter 9: Reflections on the 2020 Election

In Chapter 9 of *Melania*, titled "Reflections on the 2020 Election," former First Lady Melania Trump offers her perspective on the events surrounding the 2020 presidential election, providing insights into her personal experiences and interpretations during this period.

Themes: Distrust, Disillusionment, and Loyalty

This chapter delves into themes of distrust, disillusionment, and loyalty. Melania expresses skepticism regarding the election process, echoing sentiments of electoral irregularities. She conveys a sense of disillusionment with the media and political adversaries, suggesting a coordinated effort to undermine her husband's campaign. Throughout the narrative, her loyalty to her husband is evident, as she aligns with his perspective on the election's outcome.

Writing Style: Assertive and Personal

The writing style in this chapter is assertive and personal. Melania articulates her views with conviction, providing a candid account of her reactions to the election night developments and subsequent events. Her narrative is infused with personal anecdotes, offering readers a glimpse into her emotional state during this tumultuous time.

Author's Intentions: Justifying Beliefs and Actions

Through this chapter, Melania aims to justify her beliefs and actions during the post-election period. By sharing her perspective, she seeks to validate her skepticism of the election results and her support for her husband's refusal to concede. This narrative serves to reinforce her alignment with her husband's stance and to provide her rationale for standing by him amidst widespread controversy.

Sociopolitical Context: Election Integrity and Media Trust

The sociopolitical context of this chapter centers on debates over election integrity and media trust. Melania's reflections mirror broader discussions about the legitimacy of the 2020 election and the role of the media in shaping public perception. Her narrative contributes to the discourse on political polarization and the challenges of maintaining trust in democratic institutions.

Impact on Public Perception and Contemporary Literature

This chapter offers a rare insight into Melania Trump's personal views on a significant political event, potentially influencing public perception by humanizing her experience during the election. In contemporary literature, such firsthand accounts from political figures provide valuable perspectives on historical events, enriching the understanding of personal dynamics within political narratives.

Strengths and Weaknesses

A strength of this chapter is its candidness, as Melania openly shares her doubts and emotions regarding the election. However, a notable weakness is the lack of engagement with evidence contradicting her perspective, which may lead readers to question the completeness of her account. Additionally, the chapter may be perceived as reinforcing unsubstantiated claims, potentially impacting its credibility.

Chapter 10: The Mar-a-Lago Raid

In Chapter 10 of *Melania*, titled "The Mar-a-Lago Raid," former First Lady Melania Trump provides her personal account of the FBI's search of her residence at Mar-a-Lago in August 2022. She delves into her reactions to the event, its impact on her sense of privacy, and the broader implications she perceives for individual freedoms.

Themes: Privacy, Trust, and Civil Liberties

This chapter explores themes of privacy, trust, and civil liberties. Melania expresses profound concern over what she describes as an "invasion of privacy" by federal agents during the search of her home. She reflects on the erosion of trust between citizens and governmental institutions, emphasizing the need to safeguard individual rights against perceived governmental overreach.

Writing Style: Candid and Reflective

The writing style in this chapter is candid and reflective. Melania shares her personal feelings of anger and violation following the raid, providing readers with an intimate glimpse into her emotional response. Her narrative is introspective, as she contemplates the broader significance of the event for herself and the nation.

Author's Intentions: Highlighting Personal Impact and Broader Implications

Through this chapter, Melania aims to highlight both the personal impact of the Mar-a-Lago raid and its broader implications. By sharing her experience, she seeks to underscore the importance of protecting individual privacy and civil liberties, suggesting that her experience serves as a cautionary tale for all Americans.

Sociopolitical Context: Government Authority and Individual Rights

The sociopolitical context of this chapter centers on the balance between government authority and individual rights. Melania's account contributes to ongoing discussions about the extent of governmental power in law enforcement actions and the potential consequences for personal freedoms. Her perspective adds a personal dimension to debates about civil liberties in the context of federal investigations.

Impact on Public Perception and Contemporary Literature

This chapter offers readers a personal perspective on a high-profile federal investigation, potentially influencing public perception by humanizing the experience of those subjected to government scrutiny. In contemporary literature, such firsthand accounts provide valuable insights into the personal ramifications of political events, enriching the discourse on the intersection of personal lives and governmental actions.

Strengths and Weaknesses

A strength of this chapter is its openness, as Melania candidly shares her personal feelings and reflections on a significant and controversial event. However, a potential weakness is the limited discussion of the legal context and reasons behind the FBI's actions, which may leave readers seeking a more comprehensive understanding of the situation.

Chapter 11: The Assassination Attempt

In Chapter 11 of *Melania*, titled "The Assassination Attempt," former First Lady Melania Trump recounts a harrowing experience that threatened her husband's life during his presidency. She provides a detailed narrative of the event, her immediate reactions, and the subsequent impact on her family's sense of security.

Themes: Fear, Vulnerability, and Resilience

This chapter delves into themes of fear, vulnerability, and resilience. Melania describes the profound fear she felt upon learning of the threat against her husband's life, highlighting the inherent vulnerabilities that come with public service. She also emphasizes the resilience required to continue fulfilling her role as First Lady amidst such dangers.

Writing Style: Emotional and Reflective

The writing style in this chapter is emotional and reflective. Melania shares her personal feelings of terror and uncertainty during the incident, providing readers with an intimate glimpse into her emotional landscape. Her narrative is introspective, as she contemplates the fragility of life and the strength needed to persevere in the face of adversity.

Author's Intentions: Humanizing the First Family

Through this chapter, Melania aims to humanize the First Family by sharing a deeply personal and traumatic experience. By detailing her emotional journey during the assassination attempt, she seeks to provide readers with a more nuanced understanding of the personal sacrifices and dangers faced by those in the highest echelons of political life.

Sociopolitical Context: Security and Public Service

The sociopolitical context of this chapter centers on the security challenges inherent in public service. Melania's account contributes to discussions about the personal risks faced by political figures and their families, as well as the measures taken to protect them. Her perspective adds a personal dimension to debates about security protocols and the psychological toll of living under constant threat.

Impact on Public Perception and Contemporary Literature

This chapter offers readers a personal perspective on the dangers associated with political life, potentially influencing public perception by highlighting the human side of political figures. In contemporary literature, such firsthand accounts provide valuable insights into the personal experiences of those in power, enriching the discourse on the intersection of personal vulnerability and public duty.

Strengths and Weaknesses

A strength of this chapter is its openness, as Melania candidly shares her personal feelings and reflections on a life-threatening event. However, a potential weakness is the limited discussion of the broader implications of the assassination attempt, such as its impact on national security policies or public discourse. A more comprehensive analysis could provide readers with a deeper understanding of the event's significance.

Chapter 12: Relationships with Public Figures

In Chapter 12 of *Melania*, titled "Relationships with Public Figures," former First Lady Melania Trump offers insights into her interactions with various prominent individuals during her tenure in the White House. She reflects on the complexities of forming and maintaining these relationships within the highly scrutinized environment of political life.

Themes: Diplomacy, Public Perception, and Personal Boundaries

This chapter delves into themes of diplomacy, public perception, and personal boundaries. Melania discusses the delicate balance between her official duties and personal interactions, highlighting the importance of diplomacy in fostering positive relationships with global leaders and public figures. She also reflects on how these relationships were perceived by the public and media, and the challenges of maintaining personal boundaries amidst public scrutiny.

Writing Style: Reflective and Insightful

The writing style in this chapter is reflective and insightful. Melania provides thoughtful analyses of her interactions, offering readers a nuanced understanding of the interpersonal dynamics at play. Her narrative is introspective, shedding light on her personal experiences and the lessons she learned from engaging with various public figures.

Author's Intentions: Providing a Behind-the-Scenes Perspective

Through this chapter, Melania aims to provide readers with a behind-the-scenes perspective on her relationships with public figures. By sharing her personal experiences, she seeks to humanize these interactions and offer insights into the complexities of her role as First Lady.

Sociopolitical Context: The Role of the First Lady in International Relations

The sociopolitical context of this chapter centers on the role of the First Lady in international relations and public diplomacy. Melania's reflections contribute to discussions about the influence and responsibilities of the First Lady in shaping the nation's image and fostering diplomatic relationships.

Impact on Public Perception and Contemporary Literature

This chapter offers readers a personal perspective on the interpersonal aspects of political life, potentially influencing public perception by highlighting the relational dynamics of the First Lady's role. In contemporary literature, such narratives provide valuable insights into the personal experiences of public figures, enriching the discourse on the intersection of personal relationships and political responsibilities.

Strengths and Weaknesses

A strength of this chapter is its candidness, as Melania openly shares her personal experiences and reflections on her interactions with public figures. However, a potential weakness is the limited discussion of specific challenges or conflicts that may have arisen in these relationships, which could provide a more comprehensive understanding of the complexities involved.

Conclusion

Chapter 12 of *Melania* offers a reflective and insightful account of Melania Trump's relationships with public figures during her time as First Lady. Through her narrative, she provides readers with a nuanced understanding of the interpersonal dynamics and diplomatic responsibilities inherent in her role. While the chapter effectively conveys her personal experiences, a more detailed exploration of specific challenges in these relationships could enhance readers' understanding of the complexities involved.

Chapter 13: Media and Public Scrutiny

In *Melania*, Chapter 13, titled "Media and Public Scrutiny," former First Lady Melania Trump delves into her often complicated relationship with the press and the relentless public examination of her actions, style, and persona. She explores the ways in which media narratives shaped her image, the scrutiny she endured as the wife of one of the most polarizing presidents in modern history, and how she navigated the intense spotlight with a characteristic sense of privacy and restraint.

Themes: Misinformation, Image Control, and Public Judgment

This chapter explores themes of misinformation, the battle for image control, and the weight of public judgment. Melania reflects on the often contradictory narratives surrounding her, from being portrayed as a reluctant First Lady to accusations of being complicit in her husband's political stance. She discusses how selective reporting and speculation influenced public opinion, sometimes at odds with her own reality. The chapter also examines the struggle between staying true to oneself while operating within the constraints of public expectation and media framing.

Writing Style: Poised Yet Defiant

Melania's writing in this chapter is poised yet carries a hint of defiance. She presents herself as someone who values privacy and dignity but is also aware of the battles fought on her behalf in the media. While she refrains from engaging in direct confrontations, there is a sense of quiet resistance in her reflections, where she pushes back against certain portrayals without engaging in outright condemnation.

Author's Intentions: Reclaiming Narrative Control

With this chapter, Melania aims to reclaim control over the narrative that has often been shaped by external forces. By providing her perspective, she seeks to clarify misconceptions, counteract media distortions, and offer insight into what it was like to be scrutinized so intensely in both political and personal spheres. The chapter serves as an attempt to define herself on her own terms rather than being reduced to soundbites or caricatures.

Sociopolitical Context: Media's Role in Modern Political Life

The sociopolitical context of this chapter highlights the media's role in shaping political figures and their legacies. Melania's reflections contribute to the broader conversation about how first ladies—and women in general—are covered in the press, particularly in an era of heightened political divisions and digital media proliferation. The discussion touches on the ethical responsibilities of journalists and the blurred line between fair critique and targeted vilification.

Impact on Public Perception and Contemporary Literature

This chapter offers readers a more personal perspective on how public figures experience media scrutiny, potentially influencing public perception by humanizing the subject behind the headlines. In contemporary literature, firsthand accounts of media interaction from political figures serve as valuable case studies in the evolving relationship between power and the press. By including her voice in the conversation, Melania adds another layer to the ongoing discourse about media accountability, bias, and the responsibilities of public figures in managing their own narratives.

Strengths and Weaknesses

A strength of this chapter is its introspective approach—Melania does not merely complain about the press but attempts to analyze its impact on her life and role. However, a notable weakness is that she largely avoids deeper engagement with specific controversies where the media criticism may have been warranted. While she highlights unfair portrayals, the chapter could have benefited from a more nuanced discussion of why certain criticisms emerged and whether any had merit.

Chapter 14: Advocacy and Initiatives

In *Melania*, Chapter 14, titled "Advocacy and Initiatives," the former First Lady provides an in-depth account of her efforts to create a lasting impact beyond the traditional role of the presidential spouse. She highlights her work in public service, most notably through her *Be Best* initiative, and reflects on both the successes and challenges she faced while advocating for children's well-being, online safety, and opioid abuse awareness. This chapter offers insight into her vision for social change and the limitations of her influence within the often politically charged atmosphere of Washington.

Themes: Philanthropy, Influence, and Challenges of Public Service

The chapter explores themes of philanthropy, influence, and the challenges inherent in public service. Melania emphasizes her dedication to improving the lives of children and families, while also acknowledging the obstacles that come with promoting nonpartisan initiatives in a highly polarized political environment. She discusses how she sought to carve out a space for herself beyond her husband's presidency, emphasizing her belief in the power of kindness, empathy, and positive social engagement.

Writing Style: Purposeful and Direct

The writing style in this chapter is purposeful and direct. Melania focuses on the details of her initiatives and advocacy work, providing background on the issues she prioritized and the motivations behind her efforts. Her tone remains measured, avoiding excessive self-praise while firmly asserting her commitment to meaningful causes. She balances personal reflections with factual accounts of her engagements, illustrating both the logistical and emotional aspects of her work.

Author's Intentions: Cementing a Legacy of Compassion and Action

Through this chapter, Melania seeks to cement a legacy of compassion and action. By chronicling her efforts as First Lady, she aims to showcase the tangible impact of her initiatives while also addressing criticisms that her advocacy was overshadowed by the controversies surrounding her husband's administration. The chapter serves as both a defense of her work and a testament to the importance of focusing on issues that transcend political divisions.

Sociopolitical Context: The First Lady's Role in Policy and Social Change

The sociopolitical context of this chapter touches on the evolving role of the First Lady in shaping policy and social change. Melania's reflections contribute to broader discussions about the effectiveness of first ladies in driving meaningful progress, particularly when their platforms intersect with deeply rooted political and social challenges. Her focus on children's welfare, online civility, and opioid addiction places her within a lineage of first ladies who have championed public service causes, yet she acknowledges the difficulties of implementing initiatives in an era of hyper-partisan scrutiny.

Impact on Public Perception and Contemporary Literature

This chapter offers a more nuanced look at Melania Trump's efforts as First Lady, potentially shifting public perception by presenting her advocacy work as a serious, results-driven endeavor rather than a symbolic or superficial undertaking. In contemporary literature, first-hand accounts of advocacy efforts by political figures help to contextualize their roles beyond ceremonial duties, offering valuable insight into the real-world impact of their platforms. By documenting her experiences, Melania contributes to the historical conversation about how first ladies navigate the intersection of public service, politics, and personal ambition.

Strengths and Weaknesses

A strength of this chapter is its focus on tangible initiatives, as Melania provides clear examples of her work and the reasoning behind her chosen causes. However, a notable weakness is the absence of a more critical reflection on the limitations and reception of her initiatives. While she discusses obstacles, the chapter avoids addressing critiques regarding the scope and effectiveness of *Be Best*, particularly the contradiction between its message of online kindness and the behavior of key figures in her husband's administration. A more candid discussion of these challenges could have strengthened her argument and provided a fuller picture of her advocacy efforts.

Chapter 15: Reflections and Future Aspirations

In *Melania*, Chapter 15, titled "Reflections and Future Aspirations," the former First Lady takes a contemplative look at her time in the public eye, assessing her journey from Slovenia to the White House and beyond. With a mix of introspection and forward-looking vision, she reflects on the personal and professional lessons she has learned, the sacrifices she has made, and the legacy she hopes to leave behind. The chapter serves as a conclusion to her narrative, offering readers insight into her evolving role in the post-White House era and her aspirations for the future.

Themes: Legacy, Personal Growth, and Life Beyond the White House

This chapter revolves around the themes of legacy, personal growth, and life beyond the White House. Melania revisits defining moments from her tenure as First Lady, evaluating the impact of her work and the public's reception of her initiatives. She acknowledges the challenges of maintaining both privacy and influence while contemplating how she can continue to contribute to society in a meaningful way. Her reflections convey a sense of resilience, as she positions herself as a figure who remains steadfast in her values despite the scrutiny she has faced.

Writing Style: Poised and Reflective

The writing style in this chapter is poised and reflective, with a tone that blends gratitude, determination, and subtle defiance. Melania presents herself as someone who has navigated extraordinary circumstances with grace, choosing to focus on her inner strength rather than dwelling on past controversies. The chapter is more personal than political, with an emphasis on self-discovery and the enduring impact of her experiences.

Author's Intentions: Defining Her Own Narrative and Future Path

Melania uses this chapter to define her own narrative, ensuring that her legacy is shaped by her own words rather than media portrayals or political conjecture. She seeks to distance herself from the tumult of the Trump administration while reaffirming her commitment to select causes, hinting at potential projects, philanthropic work, or even a return to public life in a different capacity. By offering a glimpse into her aspirations, she invites readers to consider her as an independent figure rather than merely an extension of her husband's political legacy.

Sociopolitical Context: The Role of Former First Ladies in Public Life

The chapter situates Melania within the broader context of former first ladies and their evolving roles after leaving the White House. While some, like Michelle Obama and Hillary Clinton, have pursued high-profile careers in politics, media, or activism, Melania appears to lean toward a more selective and carefully curated public presence. Her reflections contribute to the discussion of how first ladies shape their post-White House identities, balancing public expectations with personal desires for privacy or continued influence.

Impact on Public Perception and Contemporary Literature

This chapter has the potential to influence public perception by positioning Melania as a reflective, forward-thinking individual who remains engaged with the world beyond her time in Washington. In contemporary literature, memoirs and political biographies often serve as tools for figures to reshape their public image, and Melania's closing reflections align with this tradition. By framing her journey as one of resilience and purpose, she seeks to leave a lasting impression on readers, even as she moves beyond the First Lady title.

Strengths and Weaknesses

A strength of this chapter is its introspective nature, allowing readers to see a more personal side of Melania that is often obscured by political narratives. Her reflections on legacy and future aspirations provide a sense of closure while also leaving the door open for continued engagement in public life. However, a potential weakness is the lack of specific details regarding her future plans. While she hints at continued advocacy and public presence, the chapter remains somewhat vague, leaving readers with more questions than concrete expectations. A clearer articulation of her next steps could have strengthened the chapter's impact.

About the Author

Callum Ellis is a thoughtful and insightful book critic passionate about exploring literature that shapes public opinion and cultural narratives. With a keen eye for detail and a balanced approach to critical analysis, Callum brings fresh perspectives to notable works, blending objective evaluation with personal reflection.

In this critical review of *MELANIA*, Callum offers readers an engaging and thought-provoking exploration of a book that dives into the life and persona of one of America's most enigmatic public figures. His work encourages readers to think beyond surface narratives and consider the complexities behind influential figures and stories.

When not reading or reviewing books, Callum enjoys engaging with thought leaders on contemporary issues and sharing insights through reviews and articles.

Made in United States
Troutdale, OR
03/16/2025